NOT

FADE

AWAY

NOT

The Rock & Roll Photography of Jim Marshall

FADE

Foreword by Michael Douglas · Edited by David Fahey

AWAY

AURUM PRESS

First published in Great Britain 1997 by
Aurum Press Limited, 25 Bedford London WCIB 3AT

First Edition

A catalogue record for this book is available from the British Library

ISBN 1 85410 525 6

Bulfinch Press is an imprint and trademark of Little, Brown and Company (Inc.)
Published simultaneously in Canada by Little, Brown & Company (Canada) Limited

Designed by John Kane
Printed and bound by Amilcare Pizzi, Milan, Italy

Jim Marshall's traveling exhibition from the *Not Fade Away* publication is sponsored by the
Hard Rock Cafe. The Hard Rock Cafe also proudly displays Mr. Marshall's photographs
as part of its worldwide collection.

The traveling exhibition from the Not Fade Away publication is printed on
Kodak Polymax Fine Art Paper.

You may look at Jim Marshall's images on the Internet: www.marshallphoto.com

Gallery Representation: Fahey/Klein Gallery,
Los Angeles 213-934-2250 (telephone), 213-934-4243 (fax)

PRINTED IN ITALY

This is my first major book. I would like to
respectfully dedicate it to . . .
the late Duane Allman
and the late Tom Jans,
who were like the brothers I never had;
and especially to my ex-wife, Rebecca Birch,
who was always there for me.
And to all the artists who trusted me and
my camera and who have given us the
music and the memories.

Acknowledgments

THERE ARE SO MANY PEOPLE I MUST THANK FOR HELPING ME IN MY CAREER AND MY life. I cannot begin to name everyone in this small space, but I would like to acknowledge a few people:

Arthur Andreas
Nancy Astor
John Berg of Columbia Records
(the late) Bert Block
(the late) Nesuhi Ertegun of Atlantic Records
Bill and Minette Farthing of Belleville, Illinois
Barry Feinstein
Kimberley Fisher
David Gahr
Dennis Gray
Marshall Lumsden of the *Saturday Evening Post*
Michelle Margetts
Jerry Stoll
George Walker
and Irwin Welcher, former owner of Compo Photo Color Service
and General Graphic Service

I'd also like to thank my printer, Kirk Anspach, who is solely responsible for making all my prints for exhibitions and for this book. My eternal thanks to Leica USA for its support and for the M2 and M4 Leicas — without them, I never could have taken these photographs. Thanks to Kodak for its high-quality film and paper, which I have used throughout my career for one simple reason — they're the best. Thanks to Charlie Casella and Steve Routhier of the Hard Rock Cafe for sponsoring the exhibition. And thanks to Karen Dane and Carol Leslie at Bulfinch Press for doing this book and taking a chance on me. Finally, special thanks to David Fahey for being my agent and helping me to make this book happen.

If I have forgotten anyone, please forgive me.

Foreword

WHEN JIM ASKED ME TO WRITE THIS PREFACE, I WAS HONORED AND DELIGHTED. I must say, however, there is perhaps no harder task than articulating the 1960s — and Jim's work — in a few succinct pages.

The standing joke, of course, is that if you remember the '60s, you weren't there. The excesses are legendary and, by and large, true. But they were excesses borne of a genuine search for truth. We didn't know what that truth looked like, but we knew there was something else out there to embrace.

Jim and I — and the myriad others (you know who you are) — are bonded eternally by the shared experience of a time when the confluence of historical, social, and political forces changed the world as we knew it. And, of course, foremost of all, there was the MUSIC, which held all the combustibles together like a familial glue.

Jim's pictures of the music makers are extraordinary for many reasons. As a human being and an artist, he has never shied away from honesty. His style is very "in your face," and yet he inspires trust and confidence in the people he photographs, and the shared intimacy is caught in the millisecond. And there it is. Forever.

There's a quality to Marshall's work that encapsulates an essence of "Hey, baby, we're all in this together. Let's try to look after one another." His images are at once larger than life and yet private and off-guard. His photographs genuinely remind us that the performers are human and, in many cases, lonely wanderers. Whether it is a glimpse of Carlos Santana meditating on a guitar riff in the middle of a Cinco de Mayo crowd, or Janis Joplin alone backstage, Jim always manages to capture the vulnerability of the performer.

No period was more powerful than the mid-'60s. I am always moved when I think of what I was doing and feeling when President Kennedy was shot. There was such a deep grief in the country and in the world, palpable everywhere. Barely three months later, the Beatles were on *The Ed Sullivan Show* and the juggernaut of the '60s was off and rolling. Music took center stage in a way it never had before.

My own life at this juncture was, to say the least, in transition. I had come out of a strict East Coast boarding school tradition and suddenly found myself in mid-'60s California — at the University of California in Santa Barbara, no less. UCSB at that time embodied a distinctly Dionysian resonance; talk about a kid in a candy store . . .

Suffice it to say, one of my more stellar accomplishments during this period was being voted Mobil Man of the Month during a brief — but clearly auspicious! — tenure as a gas station attendant.

It was an era of spirited communal living. I was ensconced in Santa Barbara at a commune we called Banana Road and going to college. We were all looking for a deeper worldview, some new way of being — of connecting, of understanding. It was a time of turning points for everyone. Women were exploring new dimensions, and Marshall McLuhan's notion of a global village was in the air. The terms were a-changin' on every level.

But the theme weaving through all of it, as ever, was the music. And there was Jim, at the heart of the action, documentarian of the folks who sang the tunes and set the tone. The accessibility of the artists represents a period of music history that will likely never be repeated. The ingenuous delight of artists, playing for the love of playing, is so evident in Jim's work.

The tenor of the (counter)culture allowed performers to open up and be seen as they were. They were not so hidden behind public relations people and managers and muscled bodyguards as they are now. It was safer then. At least for a while. It was an innocent, wonderful period, and people wanted to believe it would never end. But, as we know, the only constant of the universe is change.

In writing this introduction, I sit with a spectrum of pictures spread before me, like a huge deck of tarot cards chronicling part of my own history. I am struck by the flood of feeling and the visceral memory these photographs ignite. Music has always framed defining moments for me.

To see these pictures of people, many of whom are old friends, is like seeing snapshots of all your pals at a once-in-a-lifetime party. And I can't help but think of the ones who aren't here anymore and wonder, What if?

Who better than Jim to have been at the party to grab those moments as they sailed by. I love all these pictures — a very young Bob Dylan; the ebullient grin of Mama Cass Elliot; Jimi Hendrix and Brian Jones cruising together at the Monterey Pop Festival (another major musical turning point for rock and jazz). Perhaps, however, my favorite is the one of Janis Joplin lounging on a tattered backstage couch at some early venue. That photograph so clearly embodies the duality of public celebrity and the isolation brought on by stardom and private demons.

Jim Marshall was a part of the caravan of wonderful gypsies, visionaries, and musical pioneers. It is with pride, pleasure, and homage to an old trench buddy, as it were, that I congratulate Jim on this amazing diary of stunning musicians in a phenomenal time.

As Mick and Keith might say, I like it, like it, yes I do. And so will you.

Michael Douglas
January 1997

Introduction

I AM HONORED THAT MY PHOTOGRAPHS ARE IN THE HOMES OF SO MANY PEOPLE — that my image of an artist whose music means so much to someone is hanging on their walls. I think the images can be as important as the music because they make us remember the sound, the song, the moment.

I have been present at the birth of so many songs and great musical events, from small clubs to giant festivals, and have met many special artists. To me, the lives of these musicians I have been privileged to photograph are like the light photographers use to make images — from the soft candle-like glow of Joan Baez to the comet-like brilliance of Jimi or Janis, who flashed through our lives and burned out ever so quickly. But I think they are now lighting some other place in our universe, and their music and presence will always be a part of my life and our world.

This "career" has never been just a job — it's been my life. I have been very fortunate to have chosen my field of photography, although some days I think it chose me. I have met and walked with some of the pioneers — the giants — of jazz, blues, country, rock & roll, and folk. These musicians have all enriched our lives and the world around us.

I've been told that sometimes I am difficult to handle. However difficult I may be, in almost forty years not one lawyer, manager, artist, or agent has complained about where my work was published or the image I chose. I feel that in my photographs there is a trust given by the artists. When I point the camera at somebody, there's a covenant, and I will not violate that trust.

In terms of equipment, the Leica range finder is the only camera that ever felt right in my hands. My first Leica M2 with a 50-millimeter lens I bought on time in 1959. I put $50 down and made twelve payments of $24 a month. The Leica for me is like the American Express card — I never leave home without it. It's part of me. I think that when a subject sees that you are comfortable with your tools, your cameras, he/she becomes more comfortable with you. When I work, I carry about four Leicas and maybe one other camera. I usually shoot in black-and-white, although I've done some color photography, but I cannot do both at once, because I have to think differently for each. When I shoot in black-and-white I always print the full negative with no cropping.

In terms of technique, I was always fascinated with cameras but not photography per se. I didn't know a whole lot. I'll never know what some of the real good guys know. I use available light almost exclusively and rarely use artificial lights. Early on, I didn't even know how to use lights. When I shoot, I'm pretty compulsive because I really don't like to miss anything. I'll stay up all night if that's what it takes. No darkroom manipulation is done in my printing, either. My philosophy is, if you don't have it in the camera, you ain't got it. To make a great photo, not just a snapshot, there's got to be content and enough technical expertise to be able to print it. For black-and-white, I expose for the shadow detail and let everything fall into place. I use other techniques only when they will enhance what I see in the music — and I do *see* the music.

When I'm photographing people, I don't like to give any direction. There are no hair people fussing around, no make-up artists. I'm like a reporter, only with a camera; I react to my subject in their environment, and, if it's going well, I get so immersed in it that I become one with the camera. I'm 95 percent involved in the moment, and the other 5 percent of me is working the camera, being the mechanic.

I like to photograph people when they're doing what they do best. I think a few times I've acted like the asshole superstar photographer and lost some gigs and clients. But when someone sees a picture I've taken of Merle Haggard or Alice Walker, I think what they see is the subject in the photograph and not a "Jim Marshall" signature piece. I think my style is that I don't have a style — I never do anything the same twice. When you see my pictures, it's about the person in the photograph, not me — not the guy behind the lens. I want someone to see those *people*, not *my picture* of

them. When I'm able to capture the essence of my subject and show
something of what they do or reveal who this person is, then I've achieved
what I want to do. It's such an elusive thing, and sometimes I feel like a
sniper waiting for that shot or moment to happen. It's the same discipline —
steady, aim, focus, squeeze don't jerk. I've never had any formal training,
and I don't like theatrics in photography, but I've asked a lot of questions
from other photographers like Joe Rosenthal, Jerry Stoll, Peter Breinig —
a lot of guys. I'm not afraid to ask when I don't know, and I've made a lot
of mistakes.

All the photographers I've really admired used Leicas, like Henri Cartier-
Bresson, Robert Capa, Ernst Haas, and so many others. It's interesting to me
that the men whose work I most admire were combat photographers, such as
Robert Capa and David Douglas Duncan. And others are/were some of the
great photojournalists or photo-essayists: Cartier-Bresson; Paul Fusco of
Look magazine, now of Magnum; Leonard McComb of *Life* magazine; Carl
Mydans; Dennis Stock of Magnum, whose book, *Jazz Street*, was a great
inspiration; Jerry Stoll; John Vachon of *Look* magazine; and all of the
photographers of the Farm Security Administration.

I'm not a great concept person like Timothy White or Herb Ritts or Annie
Leibovitz. I don't do that kind of work. I'm still using old mechanical
equipment. In fact, the high-tech things I own are a cell phone, a motor
drive, and one strobe setup. I have not changed with the times — if I had I'd
probably be making more money — but I like what I do, my way.

What's different about taking photographs today versus shooting in the '60s
and '70s is that there's not the same kind of access given to photographers
nowadays as there used to be. There's a real difference between shooting
someone onstage and going backstage, hanging with the band, and getting
the more personal side of the subject. These days, bands demand that
photographers show up and shoot from a particular place onstage only for
the first three songs — before the artists get sweaty — and photographing

backstage doesn't exist anymore. Or, we're told to wait an hour before going backstage, so the musicians can get cleaned up and stuff.

In fairness to the musicians, this kind of restricted access has to be borne as the result of too many photographers selling compromising, revealing shots to any kind of tabloid or print publication. I find that practice offensive. So a lot of the kinds of photographs I took in the past I can't get anymore. No one can, because bands are not granting that kind of access, and if there's no access, there are not as many revealing portraits. Being a rock & roll photographer looks easy and glamorous, but that's not true. It used to be more fun than it is now.

Too much bullshit is written about photographs and music. Let the music move you, whether to a frenzy or a peaceful place. Let it be what you want to hear — not what others say is popular. Let the photograph be one you remember — not for its technique but for its soul. Let it become a part of your life — a part of your past to help shape your future. But most of all, let the music and the photograph be something you love and will always enjoy.

Louis (Satchmo) Armstrong once said that there are two kinds of music: good and bad. That applies to photography, too.

'Nuff said.

Jim Marshall
January 1997

NOT

FADE

AWAY

Backstairs of the Boarding House club in San Francisco, 1965, after a recording session (*counterclockwise from bottom left*): Otis Spann, Willie Mae "Big Mama" Thornton, Muddy Waters, James Cotton, Luther "Guitar" Johnson Jr., Francis Clay, and Samuel Lawhorn.

MUDDY AT THE SAME SESSION at the Boarding House in 1965. He's listening to a playback of a song just recorded. He's one of the great gentlemen in the business.

4

B ACKSTAGE AT CIRCLE STAR Theater in Redwood City, California, in the early '80s with B.B. King, Albert King, and Bobby "Blue" Bland. Thank God I had black-and-white film loaded in my camera that night, because the color of the walls, the carpet, and couch were the most atrocious shit color I've seen. B.B. didn't want to be disturbed, so the dressing room was locked while we were doing the pictures. The three of them are very good friends, and they were all on the same bill that night. Why they're all laughing should be left to the imagination. B.B. King is one of the class acts in the business.

T-BONE WALKER WAS ONE of the seminal influences in blues and rock guitar. He used to play in a San Francisco club called The Gold Mirror, which was four doors down from my uncle's store, and I remember sneaking into the bar as a teenager to see T-Bone play.

This shot was taken for ABC Records for producer Bob Thiele at a recording session in Los Angeles, spring 1967. That day I was using these battery-powered strobe lights called Mighty Lights that all the *Life* magazine guys were using. When I asked T-Bone whether the lights bothered him, he said, "No, boy, they don't bother me. When I was startin' out back in Texas, they'd put chicken wire between the stage and the audience, so we wouldn't get hit with the bottles and glasses and stuff. Well, one night this old boy comes in after shooting somebody, and the manager told us to keep playing. So we played all night until the old boy passed out and the police picked him up. So, you see, boy . . . them lights don't bother me none." One of T-Bone's most famous songs was "Stormy Monday Blues," which has been recorded by many other rock & roll musicians. He was a very influential guitar player.

J OHN LEE HOOKER AT HOME IN Redwood City, California, for *Guitar Player* magazine, 1994. The first time I saw The Hook perform was in 1963 at the Newport Folk Festival, Rhode Island. It was one of his first major appearances in front of a large, white folk audience, and it was a pretty stunning performance. He's still playing even though he's got to be close to eighty now. I think he's great.

Howlin' Wolf, Ann Arbor Blues Festival, 1969. One of the greatest blues artists of all time and an awesome performer. One of his albums, *The London Sessions*, recorded in 1971, featured Ringo Starr, Eric Clapton, Charlie Watts, Bill Wyman, and Steve Winwood. I never knew him well, but I didn't find him very gracious.

8

BILL HALEY AT MADISON
Square Garden during a
rock & roll revival show,
late August 1969. I never
photographed him other
than this one time, but Bill
Haley and His Comets, best
known for their song "Rock
Around the Clock," certainly
deserve their place in rock &
roll history.

ONE OF THE FIRST MAJOR ROCK
& roll shows in San
Francisco, 1960. On the
bill were Gene Pitney, Gene
"Duke of Earl" Chandler,
Chubby Checker, and Bobby
Freeman. This is Chubby
Checker doing the twist,
and it was one of the first
live rock & roll shows I
ever photographed. The
show was put on by Tom
Donohue, who also
organized the last Beatles
concert.

I DON'T KNOW LITTLE RICHARD
at all, but, God knows,
there's only one Little
Richard. He seems like a
very nice man. This was
taken backstage at the San
Francisco Civic Center in
1971. The show headlined
Little Richard, Chuck Berry,
and Bo Diddley. I wanted to
do a portrait of the three of
them together, but Chuck
didn't want to do it, so I
never got the shot.

THE EVERLY BROTHERS AT THE
Newport Folk Festival in
Rhode Island, July 20, 1969.
Earlier that day, an
announcement was made
at the festival about Neil
Armstrong and Buzz Aldrin
landing on the moon. Phil
and Don Everly are among
the pioneers of rock & roll.

Late August 1969 in
Madison Square Garden at
a rock & roll revival show.
I don't know Chuck Berry
very well, but he's the
ultimate showman and has
a distinctive guitar style
and stage presence. Chuck,
like many of the R&B guys,
has been a tremendous
influence.

Carl Perkins, backstage at
the Newport Folk Festival,
Rhode Island, 1969. Carl is a
real gentleman and wrote
the rockabilly anthem "Blue
Suede Shoes," which was
recorded by Elvis Presley
and many others.

RAY CHARLES AT A RECORDING
session for Atlantic Records
in New York City, 1962.

Jᴏʜɴ Mᴀʏᴀʟʟ ʙᴀᴄᴋꜱᴛᴀɢᴇ ᴀᴛ
Winterland in San
Francisco, 1968. He was
the opening act that night
for Jimi Hendrix and Janis
Joplin. Mayall is known
as the father of the British
blues, along with Alexis
Korner.

ALEXIS KORNER DISCOVERED
more musicians than almost
anyone in the business. In
the '60s and '70s Alexis and
John Mayall both had blues
bands, and, at one time or
another, almost all the guys
from Led Zeppelin, Cream,
the Rolling Stones, and all
the other huge British bands
played with either Korner or
Mayall. Both of these men
gave a lot of young musi-
cians their education and
training. This shot of Alexis
was taken in the mid-'70s in
Los Angeles for Columbia
Records.

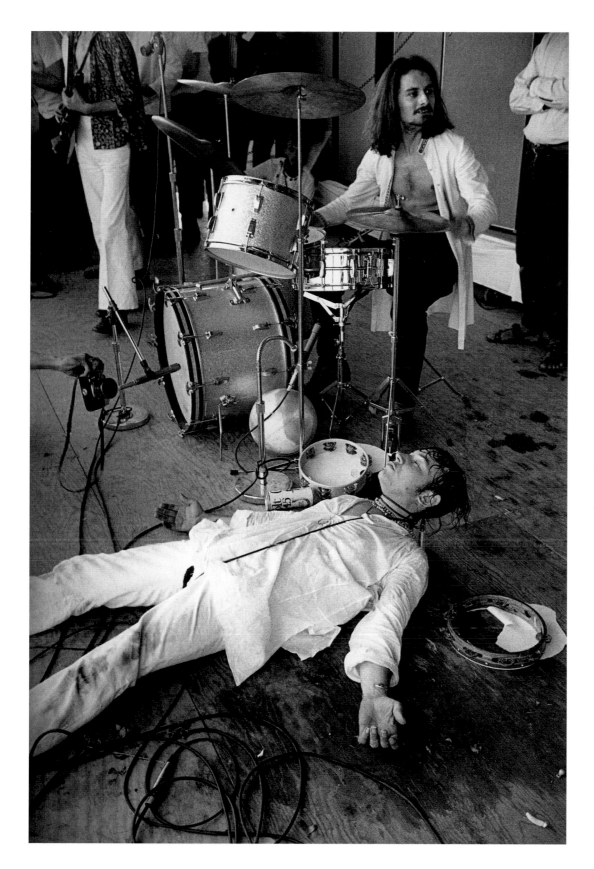

Eric Burdon at the Newport Pop Festival, California, 1968. It was a blisteringly hot day, and I was onstage right next to Eric and watched him just lie down as the roadies threw water on him. I had met Eric a couple years before this, during the first British Invasion when he came over with the band the Animals.

18

Jeff Beck in San Jose, California, 1978. Jeff's a car freak like I am, and we drove to San Jose in my Shelby Mustang. Just past Candlestick Park, I got pulled over and ticketed by this gorgeous six-foot-tall highway patrol lady. A couple hours later, when we got to the arena, they wouldn't let us in the parking lot. It was just one of those days.

K EITH MOON AT THE SAN
Francisco Civic Auditorium,
1972.

THIS IS PETE TOWNSHEND,
dawn at Woodstock.
They had been playing
half the night.

JOHN ENTWISTLE AND ROGER
Daltrey at Woodstock, 1969.

22

THE WHO IN SAN FRANCISCO,
1967. This was one of the
first published photographs
of the band in the United
States and was used in *Teen
Set*, a magazine edited by a
very special lady, the late
Judy Sims. I took this frame
outside their motel and
asked them to look straight
into the camera.

Cream in the Sausalito
Hotel stairwell, 1967. Jack
Bruce, Ginger Baker, and
Eric Clapton in one of their
first photos taken in the
United States.

24

I MET ERIC CLAPTON IN 1967
and took this picture
in 1970. He's one of the
real class acts of the music
world — someone who cares
about the roots of the music.
This is a performance shot
that shows some of
Clapton's intensity and
feeling for the music.

SKIP JAMES, A FOLK BLUES musician, at the Newport Folk Festival, Rhode Island, 1964. Many of the older blues men played at the festival that weekend, including Bukka White, Walter "Furry" Lewis, and Yank Rachel. Skip wrote a song called "I'm So Glad," which Cream had a big hit with in the late '60s. And God bless Eric Clapton because he made sure that the record company paid Mr. James the royalties due to him. The song was probably in the public domain, but Eric saw to it that Skip was paid his writer's fee. Skip James, along with other guys like John Lee Hooker, Howlin' Wolf, T-Bone Walker, and Muddy Waters, is part of the bedrock of rock & roll music.

JIMI HENDRIX AND BUDDY
Miles at Golden Gate Park,
San Francisco, during a free
concert organized by Bill
Graham, July 1967. Buddy
Miles was the drummer for
the Electric Flag and then
later for the Band of Gypsys.

AL KOOPER AND JIMI AT Monterey Pop, 1967. Al told me later that Jimi had asked him if he'd like to play the organ when Jimi did "Like a Rolling Stone," written by Bob Dylan. At the time, Al didn't think it would be appropriate, since he had recorded the song on Dylan's album *Blonde on Blonde*.

But Al said later, "To my everlasting chagrin, I told Jimi it wouldn't be appropriate. Little did I know that I'd be caught forever on camera saying I didn't want to play with Hendrix."

THIS SHOT OF JIMI WAS TAKEN during a sound check at the Monterey Pop Festival, 1967. Hendrix was playing to an empty arena — or, more accurately, to himself. I was one of the official photographers and, for some reason, everyone was at dinner except Al Kooper, Jimi's band and crew, and some of the other stagehands. I approached Jimi and told him my name was Jim Marshall — that I was one of the photographers. He made some comment like, "Far out, man, maybe this shit is supposed to be," and I asked what he meant. He said that the dude who made his amps was named Jim Marshall, and smart-ass me says, "Yeah, I know that." But then he said, "What you don't know is that my middle name is Marshall." We were all pretty stoned (the amp Marshall wasn't there), but there were three Marshalls onstage at once.

Backstage at the Monterey
Pop Festival, June 17, 1967.
Brian Jones and Jimi were
just wandering around
together. Imagine, two stars
of their stature being able to
do that at a concert today.
I was on assignment for
Esquire and *Teen Set*
magazines, and a few record
companies. This was Jimi's
first U.S. concert date.

Another shot of Jimi during the same sound check at Monterey Pop. Jimi hit a note on his guitar, and the way it made him feel is all over his face. I was three feet from him and shot this with a Leica M2, with a medium-wide angle lens. I don't know how many people really knew Jimi — he had arrogance, sex appeal, and more talent and excitement than any one man has a right to.

An interesting shot of Jimi frizzing Noel Redding's hair backstage at Winterland, 1968.

Golden Gate Street
rehearsal studios in San
Francisco, 1967. I asked
Janis Joplin and Big Brother
(*from left:* Sam Andrew,
Peter Albin, Janis, David
Getz, and James Gurley) if
they wanted to do a silly
'50s shot. We were just kids
having some fun.

JANIS JOPLIN WAS SUCH AN important part of my photographic life. To be able to know and photograph someone who gave so totally of herself onstage is a rare feeling. I felt that I could take pictures of Janis at almost any time — she was so real, and she loved the camera. This shot was taken in 1966 in San Francisco at the Golden Gate Park panhandle section. There's an innocence to this portrait, and it shows Janis's beginnings, before big stardom and success hit.

THIS PORTRAIT WAS TAKEN OF
Janis in Golden Gate Park, a
year and one-half later, in
1968. Janis is clearly famous
now, a bona fide star, and
the crowd is all around her.

THESE TWO JOPLIN photographs with the Southern Comfort bottle have a mystery about them. They were shot in 1968 backstage at San Francisco's Winterland — both taken with the same camera and lens, but different rolls. I did not number my rolls in order that night, and to this day I do not know which was taken first. When I showed Janis the picture of her lying back with the bottle in her hand, she said, "Jim, this is how it is sometimes. Lousy." Some people said I shouldn't have published the picture of her lying back with the bottle in her hand, but I'll defend it to the death. It's an honest picture, and Janis liked it. Janis was a great subject to photograph, because she was not afraid of the camera and came alive onstage — that was her world. She was very real and still a little girl when she died, a very famous little girl.

Tʜɪs sʜᴏᴛ ᴏꜰ Gʀᴀᴄᴇ Sʟɪᴄᴋ
and Janis was taken in 1967
for *Teen Set* magazine for an
article on the "Two Queen
Bees of San Francisco
Rock." That morning I went
over to Grace's house and
then had to leave and pick
up Janis. Janis wasn't in the
mood to do any pictures
that day, but I begged her
and she came along.
Everyone always thought
there was a huge rivalry
between Janis and Grace,
but they were dear friends.
This is the only time they
were ever photographed
together, and by the end of
the session, we were all
getting pretty silly and
clowning around.

THIS IMAGE BECAME A VERY famous picture and poster of the Jefferson Airplane [*above*] at Golden Gate Park, San Francisco, 1967, taken for *Look* magazine. Clockwise from the bottom, there's Grace Slick, Jorma Kaukonen, Spencer Dryden, Jack Casady, Marty Balin, and Paul Kantner. I took the picture from underneath them all — with a 21-millimeter lens on a Leica M4 with no reflector — because I thought it would be far out.

BUFFALO SPRINGFIELD [*right*] in Ghirardelli Square in San Francisco, about 1968. This is just a bunch of guys goofing around (*clockwise from the bottom*): Dewey Martin, Stephen Stills, Neil Young, Richie Furay, and Bruce Palmer.

Neil Young at the first
Crosby, Stills, Nash and
Young recording session in
Los Angeles, 1969.

Jerry Garcia was one of the
most accessible of all the
artists I've shot. I knew
Jerry almost from day one
with the Grateful Dead, and
there were never any
conditions about taking his
picture. This was taken at
the first Crosby, Stills, Nash
and Young recording session
in 1969.

GRACE SLICK AND DAVID
Crosby, taken in front of
Vesuvio's Café on Columbus
Avenue in San Francisco,
1970. We were just hanging
out together. David saw the
sign and looked at it in a
way that showed his sense
of humor.

A VERY YOUNG DAVID CROSBY
backstage at the Circle Star
Theatre in the San Fernando
Valley, 1965 or 1966.

T HE DAY I TOOK THIS SHOT IN
1967 those bastards from the
band dosed me on acid. All
I remember is that it was
taken in San Francisco
across the street from
Enrico's Coffee House. It's
one of the quintessential
Dead shots I have, taken in
natural light (*clockwise from
the left:* Jerry Garcia, Bill
Kreutzmann, Pigpen, Bob
Weir, and Mickey Hart, and
Phil Lesh in the center).

Dead End photo of Jerry
Garcia, taken backstage at
Woodstock, 1969. The sign
was not placed there by
anyone — it was exactly
right where you see it and
made for a cool shot.

Publicity shot of Country Joe
and the Fish (Barry Melton,
David Cohen, Bruce Barthol,
Country Joe McDonald, and
Chicken Hirsch), taken in
Berkeley, 1968.

Moby Grape (Skip Spence, Jerry Miller, Bob Mosley, Peter Lewis, Don Stevenson) in Los Angeles for Columbia Records, 1968. In 1967, I took a photo of Moby Grape for their self-titled first album, which showed Don Stevenson flipping the bird — way before that kind of thing became common. Well, the first printing of the Moby Grape album went out, and by the second printing, the extended middle finger magically disappeared — by the studio's demand and the technical wizardry of airbrushing.

C APTAIN BEEFHEART
(aka Don Van Vliet) [*left*] at
his place in Santa Cruz in
the early '70s for the *LA
Times Sunday Magazine*.

D R. JOHN (AKA MALCOLM
"Mac" Rebennack) [*above*]
in his gris-gris days,
backstage at the Boarding
House, San Francisco, 1983.

Joni Mitchell at home in Laurel Canyon, 1969, for *Look* magazine. It wasn't the most fun shoot I've ever completed — her managers tried to stage and control everything. All the controls and bullshit cost Joni the *Look* cover.

I've photographed Joni about four different times over her career, and, in terms of her body of work and musical gifts, she is second to no one.

J IM MORRISON AT THE
Northern California Folk
Rock Festival in San Jose,
1968. I don't think I ever
spoke three words to
Morrison. We were on the
side of the stage, and I was
shooting with just one frame
left on the roll, and Jim said,
"Hey, Marshall, you want a
photo?" and looked right
into my camera. He was one
of those guys in his own
space. I never got close to
him. My impression of
Morrison was that he was
like C. S. Lewis, spiritual
without being religious.

Rₐₙᴅʏ Nᴇᴡᴍᴀɴ [*left*] ᴀᴛ ʜɪs home in southern California for *Rolling Stone*, 1973. I never knew Randy well, but I think he's written some great songs.

Fʀᴇᴅ Nᴇɪʟ's ᴘʟᴀᴄᴇ ɪɴ ʀᴏᴄᴋ & roll history is twofold — first as a folk performer and then as a songwriter. He used to have conniptions at times, like the night he was performing at a club in the Village and said to the crowd, "I'm going to go tune this thing up." The next thing we heard was this big crash when Freddy smashed his twelve-string into a tree. He wrote this great song called "The Dolphins" and has a lot of humor in his songs. This image [*above*] was taken at a club in New York City. I've not seen him in twenty years, but I love him. He also wrote "Everybody's Talking."

Aseventeen-year-old
Jackson Browne [*above*] at
his first demo session in 1965
at Columbia Recording
Studios in Los Angeles.

This photograph of Kris
Kristofferson [*right*] was
taken in late 1970 or early
1971 in Los Angeles at the
Continental Hyatt House on
Sunset Boulevard, which
was owned at the time by
Gene Autry. I met Kris in
early 1969, before his first
album had come out, and I
came back to San Francisco
from Nashville shell-shocked
after hearing songs like "Me
and Bobby McGee,"

"Sunday Morning Coming
Down," "For the Good
Times," and "Jody and the
Kid." The guy was brilliant.
Since then we've been good
friends, and I've done two or
three of the jackets for Kris's
albums.

The year Kris came on the
scene, nobody knew who he
was, and I remember talking

to Barry Olivier, who ran the Berkeley Folk Festival, about putting Kris on between sets. I was telling my then wife-to-be, Rebecca, and everyone I knew to come out and hear this guy! Kris did three songs at Berkeley, and at the end the audience was just stunned and then went nuts with applause. Later I spoke to Johnny Cash and one of

the organizers about getting Kris onstage at the Newport Folk Festival in Rhode Island in 1969. During that same year he wasn't allowed to play between the set changes at the Big Sur Folk Festival, but the next year, in 1970, he was a headliner when Big Sur moved to the Monterey County Fairgrounds.

This picture was shot on a Sunday morning. It's a very personal picture. I've got maybe one hundred rolls on Kris, and the motherfucker doesn't take a bad shot. From every angle this guy is such a good-looking man, he's got such charm about him. It's really hard to take a bad picture of Kris.

SINGER AND SONGWRITER TIM Hardin hit the scene during the early '60s. This is a funny picture, the last frame on a roll, taken in 1964 at 42nd Street and Seventh Avenue in New York City. Tim was a folk-blues musician, but he wrote "If I Were a Carpenter," "Reason to Believe," and "Misty Roses," and a lot of people in rock & roll have recorded his songs. He was a very important songwriter, and unfortunately he died a few years after this shot was taken.

THIS IS A VERY IMPORTANT
photograph to me. It's a
picture of the late Steve
Goodman taken in 1983 in
Eugene, Oregon. Steve was
playing a Johnny Cash show
there and died within the
year from leukemia. This
picture hurts me a lot. Steve
was a really great writer, his
most famous song being
"The City of New Orleans,"
which was recorded by Arlo

Guthrie. I was conspicuously
not taking pictures of Steve
at this concert because all
his hair was gone from the
chemotherapy treatments. I
had pictures of him at the
Bread & Roses Festival from
three years before and had
known him for years. I
remember Steve came over
to me and said, "Hey,

Jimmy, I know you're not
taking pictures of me
because of the way I look,
but it's okay, man. I'd like
to be in your book some-
day." He knew he was
dying. I said to him, "If
you're not in the book,
there won't be a book." I
promised. He was one of the
real good guys and a good
friend.

IN THE EARLY '70S, I MET TOM Jans when he was going out with Mimi Fariña, Joan Baez's younger sister. He wrote a lot of great country-and-western songs, like "Loving Arms," "Heart's Island," "My Mother's Eyes," and "Marguerita." I helped to get some of his early stuff recorded. His songs have been recorded by Elvis Presley, Barbra Streisand, Bette Midler, and others. He once referred to me as "the Gertrude Stein of the San Francisco music scene," because so many people used to write music and crash at my place. Tommy died in a motorcycle accident in the late '70s. He was a close friend, a brother, and a great songwriter.

Jimmy Buffet backstage at the now defunct Boarding House club, San Francisco, in 1975. My favorite corner in that room was where this shot was taken. And I'm going to tell you something about Jimmy Buffet — he is interested in the environmental movement and other worthy causes, but he knows people are paying good money to come to his concerts. When you're at a Buffet show, you can forget your troubles for two hours and come out feeling really good. Jimmy knows he's a performer, and people are coming to hear him sing, not preach. I've been very lucky because I'll never photograph someone I don't like, and Jimmy is someone I really like to photograph. This shot was taken over twenty years ago, but I just photographed him two years ago for a CD package, and it was just as easy.

64

KENNY LOGGINS AND JIM
Messina in Los Angeles,
1972. I was shooting them
for Columbia Records, and
I knew Jim from his Buffalo
Springfield days.

Sonny and Cher, backstage at the Cow Palace in San Francisco, 1965. I didn't know either Sonny or Cher very well. This was taken at the time that "I Got You Babe" was number one on the charts. I like this picture because it's without any of the posing — without all the glamour crap.

D ENNY DOHERTY AND JOHN
Phillips [*left*] of the Mamas
and the Papas at the
Fairmont Hotel in San
Francisco, 1967.

M AMA CASS ELLIOT AND
Michelle Phillips [*above*] of
the Mamas and the Papas
on a tour plane, 1967. I
think this is a really sweet
photo.

Mama Cass Elliot at the Fairmont Hotel in San Francisco for the *Saturday Evening Post*, 1967. She was one of the really very special people. I recently met her daughter, Owen, and she told me how much she likes my photos of her mom. That is very important to me.

Opening day Woodstock, 1969. Richie Havens was the first performer of the day. I remember his manager didn't want him to be photographed because of some paranoid hippie idea about the establishment. I suggested to the manager to let them film Richie's performance anyway because (we knew) this would never happen again. Well, the rest is history. Richie opened Woodstock and just set the tone for the event. His performance there is a piece of rock & roll history.

COUNTRY JOE MCDONALD JUST
before he went onstage at
Woodstock to perform his
now famous "F - U - C - K"
cheer.

G RAHAM NASH, JONI
Mitchell, unknown, John
Sebastian, Stephen Stills,
Joan Baez, Dorothy
Morrison, and some gospel
singers whose names I
forget, taken at the Big Sur
Folk Festival in 1969.

Otis Redding at the
Monterey Pop Festival, June
16, 1967. Otis was a big guy
at six feet, two inches, and
quite a performer. On this
night in Monterey, he came
out in a lime green suit and
gave the single-greatest
performance I've seen in my
life. Later that evening, the
late Brian Jones from the
Stones and I were standing
backstage, and Brian said,
"You know, Jim, I think
Mick is the best performer
in the world, and I think
we've got the best band, but
you couldn't give me a
million quid to follow Otis
Redding onstage." Anyway,
Otis came out at a hundred
miles an hour with Booker
T. and the MG's and the
Mar-Keys, and I was about
four feet away from them
the whole show. Less than
six months later Otis was
killed in a plane crash in
Wisconsin, just before
"(Sittin' on) The Dock
of the Bay" became a
really big hit.

Miss Aretha Franklin in
Las Vegas for Atlantic
Records, 1970. What else can
I say about Aretha? She's
one of the magical
performers.

74

THE BEATLES [*left*] COMING off the plane on August 29, 1966, before their last concert.

JOHN LENNON [*above*] backstage prior to the Candlestick concert.

THE BEATLES COMING ONTO THE stage of their last concert ever, August 29, 1966, in Candlestick Park, San Francisco. I was the only photographer allowed backstage. When we arrived at the stadium, the band was in an armored car, and I was in another car following, and the old fart groundskeeper at the center field gate wouldn't let us in — he didn't know what was going on! So we had to drive around this pretty hardcore ghetto, Hunter's Point, while things got straightened out, and we finally got in about twenty minutes later.

It did not feel like a momentous occasion — the stadium wasn't even full and the noise from the fans was tremendous. The Beatles couldn't even hear themselves. It was just another concert, although it turned out to be a piece of history. The whole day was very much like out of *A Hard Day's Night*.

Paul and John onstage
at Candlestick Park.

Ringo at Candlestick
Park on August 29, 1966.

Oₙₑ ᴏꜰ ᴍʏ ᴍᴏsᴛ ɪɴᴛᴇʀᴇsᴛɪɴɢ and uncommon shots of a young Bob Dylan, taken in 1965 at a very famous press conference at KQED-TV. This is a rare one of Bobby smiling.

Wнат ᴅɪᴅ Cнᴜʀᴄнɪʟʟ ꜱᴀʏ about Russia? A riddle wrapped in a mystery inside an enigma? Well, Dylan is like that. This particular photo was taken one Sunday morning when Bobby, his girlfriend Suze Rotolo, Dave Van Ronk, and Terri Van

Ronk all were going to breakfast in New York. Just two frames were shot — no big deal — but I feel it shows Bob was still a kid in 1963. Contrary to popular belief, this shot did not inspire the song "Like a Rolling Stone." No one really knows where he was

coming from, but he's one of the most brilliant songwriters of our time. The last time I photographed him was in 1980.

Bob Dylan and Joan Baez poolside at the Hotel Viking in Newport, Rhode Island, 1964. The hat that Joan is wearing is mine, which looked better on her than on me. Bobby and Joan were definitely an item at this point and played together at the Newport Folk Festival.

ROBBIE ROBERTSON, MICHAEL
McClure, Bob Dylan, and
Allen Ginsberg in a San
Francisco alley now named
Kerouac Strasse. I was just
hanging out nearby shooting
on this day in 1965. This
was taken just at the time of
Dylan's first electric tour.

Paul Simon in Ocean Beach, California, 1971. We had dinner at my mom's house that night. He's one of the great songwriters of all time.

Aʀᴛ Gᴀʀꜰᴜɴᴋᴇʟ ꜰᴏʀ ʜɪꜱ
first solo album for
Columbia, *Angel Clare*, at
Enrico's Coffee House in
San Francisco, 1973. When
Angel Clare went gold, Art
sent me the gold record
himself. Artie has always
been very particular about
what pictures he'll allow of
himself to be published. I
think this is really a nice
shot.

D R. HOOK AND THE MEDICINE
Show (*clockwise from far
left:* Jance Garfat, George
Cummings, Richard Elswit,
William Francis, Dennis
Locorriere, Ray Sawyer/Dr.
Hook, John "Jay" David)
was a great band from New
Jersey. This picture was
taken in my living room
in the mid-'70s in San
Francisco, and I had shot
two or three album covers
for the band. Some of their
songs were just hilariously
funny.

The Electric Flag band
was started by Michael
Bloomfield in 1967. This
shot of band members
Harvey Brooks, Herbie Rich,
Mike Bloomfield, Buddy
Miles, Peter Strazza, Barry
Goldberg, Nick Gravenites,
and Marcus Doubleday was
taken in Sausalito for the
back of their first album
cover for Columbia Records,
1968.

MICHAEL BLOOMFIELD OF the group The Electric Flag. lying on the floor recording *Super Session*, at Columbia Records Studio in Los Angeles, 1968. Michael was probably one of the most pure guitar players in the business. You could play *any* blues record for Michael and he could tell you who was playing, who mastered it, who recorded it, and where it was done. He played with Paul Butterfield and he was also the first guitarist to play with Bob Dylan, when Dylan went electric. He just loved to play and died too young.

Michael Bloomfield listening to a playback at Columbia Studios in San Francisco, 1973. This photo was used in the album package for *Triumvirate* with Dr. John, Michael Bloomfield, and John Hammond Jr.

THIS SHOT OF THE ALLMAN Brothers Band was taken in Macon, Georgia, in 1969 for the cover of *At Fillmore East.* From the left, Jai Johanny Johanson, Duane, Gregg, Dickey Betts, Berry Oakley, and Butch Trucks. Now, the interesting part of this story is that I hear there are guided tours of the Lower East Side in New York City that supposedly visit the spot where this shot was taken. None of the pictures on the *At Fillmore East* album or CD packages were taken at the Fillmore East. Right before we did the shot in Macon, I stenciled "The Allman Brothers Band at Fillmore East" on one of the cases. For the album concept, I received a platinum record from the Allman Brothers' current manager.

There are two stories about why the band is laughing. As best we could tell, I had the only cocaine in Macon, Georgia, that day. So what I remember saying is, "I want one shot laughing — no laughing, no dope." But the other story is that somebody farted.

UANE ALLMAN IN SAN
Francisco, 1969. There's not
a lot I can say about Duane
Allman without writing
volumes. In all my life there
are few people I've met like
him. When I did the album
cover for *At Fillmore East*,
he told the record company
that he wanted me to do it
my way, no restrictions. It's
really hard to talk about this
kid. This shot was taken in
the bathroom of the Holiday
Inn before Duane, my ex-
wife, Rebecca, and I ate
dinner at my mom's place —
the rest of the band ate in
the hotel and got sick.

To me, the soul of the
Allman Brothers Band died
when Duane passed away.
The day he died, I walked
the streets of San Francisco
for about fourteen hours.
This is a kid who makes me
cry, and I still do sometimes
when I look at this picture.
He was just one of the guys.
He's been gone over twenty-
five years now, and his
music is still as fresh as it
was the day he wrote it.

Stu Cook, Doug Clifford,
and John Fogerty of
Creedence Clearwater
Revival, taken somewhere
over Memphis, Tennessee, in
a Lear jet, 1971. I did two
tours with Creedence, and
this was taken just when the
band had become a trio,
after Tom Fogerty left. The
pilot had just done a three-
hundred-sixty-degree roll,
and this is one of my
favorite shots of all time.

S LY STONE IS ONE OF THE
most charismatic of all the
performers I've met. He
could light up a concert hall
with his smile. This was
taken in 1978.

Frampton comes alive, taken in the early '70s for Peter's Oakland Coliseum concert put on by Bill Graham, "A Day on the Green."

JOHNNY WINTER WITH OTHER
musicians in a dressing
room at the Memphis Blues
Festival, 1969.

Rick Derringer, Boz
Scaggs, and Les Dudek in
Oakland, 1971.

MALIBU, CALIFORNIA, AT THE ranch of Booker T. Jones, 1974. Booker has played on some of the greatest records of all time and probably is the best keyboard player in rock & roll and rhythm & blues history.

Buddy Guy and Junior Wells
at the Ann Arbor Blues
Festival, 1969. Before
wireless microphones and
transmitters, musicians
would walk out into the
audience with these long
hundred-foot cords. To get
this picture I was walking
right behind Buddy and
Junior through the audience.
I used a Leica with a 21-
millimeter lens. I like the
picture because of the
energy between the two of
them.

I TOOK THIS PICTURE OF THE late Minnie Riperton for an album she was completing for Columbia Records in the late '70s. This was shot right near Shelley's Manhole in Los Angeles. Minnie was really sweet and very gracious. As it happens, a couple of years ago I visited her widower, Dick Rudolph, at the record company he presides over. The receptionist was this young kid, and I happened to mention while I was waiting for Dick that I thought Minnie was one of the greatest ladies I had ever met and what a loss it was when she passed. And then Dick comes out and says, "I'd like to introduce you to my son." His son, of course, was the receptionist, and he turned to me and said, "Thanks for saying all those lovely things about my mom."

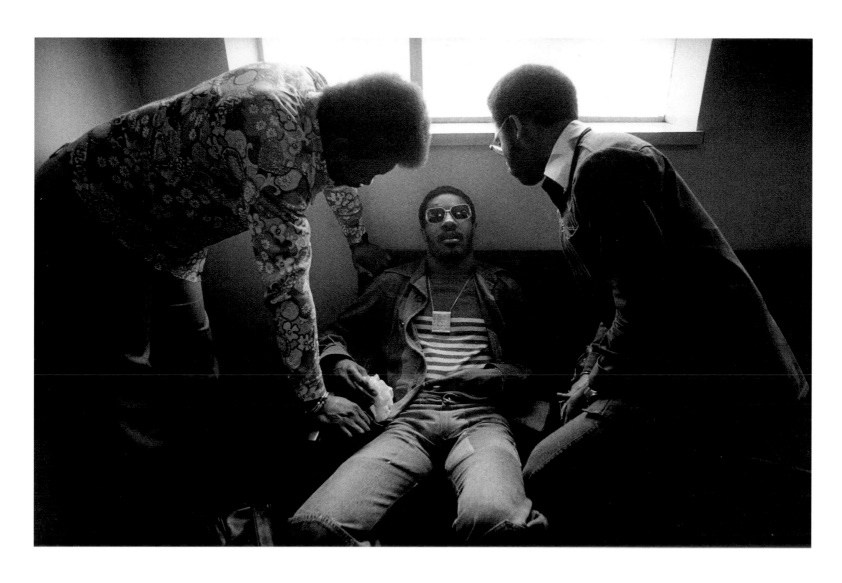

Stevie Wonder at the Circle
Star Theater in Redwood
City, California, 1972.

Alice Cooper (aka Vincent Furnier) backstage in Denver, 1972. I was on tour with Alice in the '70s and, as I recall, it was a really well organized tour. Every day around four o'clock in the afternoon, Vincent Furnier metamorphosed into Alice — so that by showtime he was *Alice Cooper*! I could never figure out how a guy could drink that much beer and still be skinny.

Outside Johnny Cash's
recording studio in
Hendersonville, Tennessee,
in about 1974. You can see
how comfortable Waylon
Jennings and Johnny are
together. These are two
friends hanging out together.

Folsom Prison in California, 1969. I've done about four or five album covers for Johnny Cash. On this day John was recording a live album for Columbia Records. The granite walls in Folsom are about eight feet thick, and we had just gotten off the bus and gone through one giant gate into a holding area. Then we went through a second gate, and, when it clanked shut, John said, "Jim, there's a feeling of permanence in that sound." After that, I started wondering when we were going to get out of there.

JOHNNY FLIPPING THE BIRD AT San Quentin Prison, 1970. Contrary to popular belief, John has never been in prison. I think he got busted once for being drunk or something when he was a kid — I don't know and it's not my business — but he's never been in jail. I've known John since 1962, and I forget why he flipped the bird in this picture — it might have been directed at the television crew who was filming there, or I might have suggested doing a special shot for the warden — but for whatever reason, this has become a very famous, iconic picture. His record company is still using it. It shows John's individuality, but the gesture was definitely done in jest. John's got a great sense of humor and this was not a serious shot.

JOHNNY CASH AND JUNE CARTER listening to music in Hendersonville, Tennessee, 1969. I'll tell you right now, I would lie in front of a truck for June Carter. She's a lady who is elegant, a brilliant writer, a great performer, and I don't know if John wants to hear this, but I think she saved John's life. If two people were destined to be together, it would have to be Johnny Cash and June Carter.

WAYLON JENNINGS BACKSTAGE at the Boarding House in San Francisco, 1975 or 1976. One of Waylon's greatest albums is *Honky Tonk Heroes*, in which all the songs but one were written by Billy Joe Shaver, with the exception of "We Had It All," written by Troy Seals and Donny Fritts. His choice of material has always been great, and one of the reasons why I love him is that he's a fucking outlaw, like me. He does it all his way.

MERLE HAGGARD NEAR Redwood City, California, 1978. I don't remember why I was there, but Merle and I were on his bus listening to the first playback of the song "I'm Always on the Mountain When I Fall," which Merle recorded with Bonnie Owens. It's a beautiful song. Merle used one of these shots on his album called *From Graceland to the Promised Land: My Tribute to Elvis Presley*.

Now, that afternoon I was going to a concert that Kris Kristofferson and Willie Nelson were doing at Stanford, and Merle asked if he could come along. Later that night we arrived backstage, with Merle carrying his guitar without a case, where some security asshole wouldn't let Merle in because he didn't have a pass. Finally one of Willie's hands showed up to let Merle in and said to the security guy, "Hey, the man's *face* is his pass." Once we were backstage, Merle sat in with Kris and Willie and played backup. All three of those guys are real gentlemen.

Roy Buchanan in the late '70s. This is one of my "studio" shots, except that all my studios are always hotel rooms. Roy committed suicide in 1988. He got busted for something and hung himself in jail. He was one of the most important blues guitar players and was once called "the best unknown guitarist in the world." He's influenced generations of musicians. I think this is a very haunting picture.

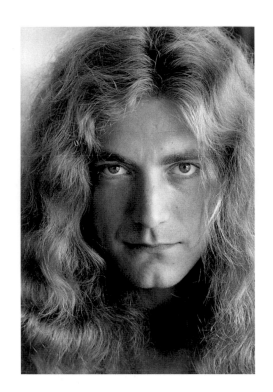

Window-lit shot of Led
Zeppelin lead guitarist
Jimmy Page [*upper left*] at
the Continental Hyatt House
on Sunset Boulevard in 1970.

Led Zeppelin bass player
John Paul Jones [*lower left*]
at the Continental Hyatt
House, 1970.

ANOTHER WINDOW SHOT OF Led Zeppelin lead singer Robert Plant [*opposite, upper right*] from the same day. An intense young man.

JOHN BONHAM [*opposite, lower right*] at the Continental Hyatt House, 1970. This was taken at the same time as the other three Led Zeppelin portraits, but

John didn't want to stand next to the window, so I shot it with slightly different lighting. He was a really funny guy. I don't know why, but I've found that the drummers in bands are a lot of fun. John and I had our share of hotel room trashings and other wild things together.

LED ZEPPELIN BAND members John Bonham, Jimmy Page, and Robert Plant [*above*] taken from the back of a limousine on the way to a gig at the Los Angeles Forum, 1971. I think they were all really tired, and I only photographed Led Zeppelin one other time after this for Atlantic Records.

The Rolling Stones back-
stage in San Francisco, 1965.
I look at some of these old
shots and think . . . Yeah, we
were all young once.

Keith Richards during
Exile on Main Street
sessions, 1972. I think this is
one of my best photos — the
quintessential Keith photo.

Los Angeles, 1972. During the recording of *Exile on Main Street* I was given unlimited access by the Stones. I had just photographed them for *Life* magazine and knew Keith and Mick pretty well. Jagger could be in the control room and start to say something to Keith, and before the words even came out of his mouth, Keith was doing it on the guitar. I've been to a lot of sessions, but I've never seen two guys work in synch this way before.

Mick Jagger onstage in San Francisco, 1972. One of the greatest performers ever and never afraid of the camera.

MICK IN A PRIVATE MOMENT on the tour plane in 1972. The thing about Jagger that isn't obvious is that he is very aware of everything that goes on in all aspects of the tour. He's not just a great musician, he's a genius.

Dave Navarro of the Red Hot Chili Peppers, during a rehearsal break in a Los Angeles doorway. I shot the Chili Peppers for Warner Brothers in 1996, and it was one of the more difficult shoots I've ever done. No one had told the guys that there was a photo session that day, and nobody wanted to stand for pictures. I took ten rolls in two hours. Since then, Dave Navarro has become a really good friend.

Chad Smith, drummer of the Chili Peppers, 1996.

Fᴌᴇᴀ (ᴀᴋᴀ Mɪᴄʜᴀᴇʟ Bᴀʟᴢᴀʀʏ),
bassist of the Chili Peppers,
1996.

Aɴᴛʜᴏɴʏ Kɪᴇᴅɪs, ʟᴇᴀᴅ
singer of the Red Hot Chili
Peppers, 1996.

Ian Astbury, LEAD SINGER of the Cult, in an amphitheater outside Denver called Red Rocks, 1991. Ian, along with Billy Duffy, was one of the leaders of the Cult, and he has an incredible knowledge of the history of the music business. Ian cares about music — it's not just a job to him — and he's one of the really great performers. One shot [*left*] is from the stage, and the other shot [*above*] is taken from backstage at the end of a two-year tour. Ian gave me the same kind of open access to him and the Cult that bands used to allow in the '60s and '70s. Hardly any photographer ever gets that kind of access anymore, and I try to make my pictures reflect the latitude that I've been given.

GRACE SLICK ON HAIGHT
Street, 1967. Grace and
Linda Perry recorded a song
together in 1996 called
"Knock Me Out."

L INDA PERRY, FORMERLY WITH 4 Non Blondes, in her studio in San Francisco, 1996. One of the shots from these sessions was used as part of the CD package for *In Flight*.

Chris Isaak and Bonnie
Raitt at the Bammies, 1996.

NATHAN CAVALERI WAITING TO go onstage at a club in San Francisco, 1994. This twelve-year-old prodigy from Australia had already played with B.B. King, Buddy Guy, and lots of other greats. I'm sure some old black blues guy died and was born again in this kid. He plays with amazing taste and control and is a really sweet kid.

Still Crazy After All These Years

By Jon Bowermaster

JIM MARSHALL IS IN THE KITCHEN OF HIS NARROW floor-thru apartment. I'd met him only ten minutes earlier, and he'd already cracked open a fifth of his favorite Irish whiskey, John Powers, and spilled the beans: He's done a lot of cocaine in the past; he emotionally abused his second wife right out the door; and he is, by his own admission, a known madman. Marshall is not subtle.

When you enter the apartment, which lies at the fringe of San Francisco's Castro District, it takes a while to adjust to the darkness. The window shades are drawn, a hangover from Marshall's more paranoid days. A long hallway serves as both entryway and introduction to the man many regard as the best music photographer of the last thirty-five years. Janis, Jimi, Jagger, Dylan, Rita Coolidge and Kris Kristofferson, Keith Moon, Led Zeppelin, John Coltrane, Aretha Franklin, Ray Charles, Thelonious Monk — they all stare from the hallway walls, captured by Marshall's beat-up Leicas. The Rolling Stones glare from a cover of *Life*, Joan Baez from the cover of *Look*.

"What do you call this area, Jim? Your gallery?"

"Hell, it's a dirty, grungy hallway that needs its damn rug shampooed," Marshall yells from the kitchen, where he is engaged on the phone, shouting belligerently. He slams the phone down with a bang. He's a little ticked off at the moment but willing to talk about his pictures. Like, which is the most famous Jim Marshall photograph?

"Probably this one here of Janis Joplin, backstage at Winterland in 1968," he says, wandering into the hallway. "Janis loved me; I was in the dressing room just clicking away. The band knew me. Everybody knew me. 'Marshall's here, big deal.' Janis is doing some outrageous posing." He stops abruptly and stalks back into the kitchen, suddenly sullen. "Some people said I

shouldn't have published that picture of her lying back, with the bottle in her hand, but I'll defend it to the death. People said her legs looked too fat. But Janis said, 'Hey, that's a great shot because it's how it is sometimes. Lousy.' But you know, I don't really care if Janis liked the picture or not; it was an honest picture. A strong picture. It just happened that she liked it a lot."

Later that night, Marshall is back in the kitchen, working on the John Powers again. He's been out closing one of the two or three San Francisco bars that he says will still allow him through their doors. Fully fortified, he heads for the living room, through the hallway, passing the portraits from the past, a past that is still a big part of Marshall's life. Earlier, we'd watched a videotape of *Back to the Future*, and I'd asked him whether he ever wished he could go back in time, to the good old days.

"Oh, no, man," he said. "I'd go far into the future. I'd never go back."

Kris Kristofferson and Jim Marshall go way back. The photographer likes to think a Kristofferson-penned lyric from "Pilgrim Chapter Thirty-three" could have been written about him: "He's a walking contradiction, partly truth, partly fiction, takin' every wrong direction, on his lonely way back home." Several of Marshall's intimates remember him in other ways: compassionate, loud, aggressive, obnoxious, caring, racist, sensitive, ill mannered, nice guy, alienating, talented, a boor. His two favorite words are "magical" and "special," usually used in reference to the hundreds of musicians, and their music, that he worked with and loves. He's been in jail and spent years on probation. At his fiftieth birthday party, a cop, a lawyer, and a drug dealer toasted him in unison. Annie Leibovitz once called Marshall "*the* rock and roll photographer." Marshall's contemporary David Gahr says his friend of more than thirty years is "the best live-music photographer this country's ever seen."

The rock & roll photographer once broke a guy's jaw with a Leica. He has shot people and been shot, knifed people and been knifed. His third favorite word is "motherfucker." One of his favorite memories from over thirty years spent in the rarefied company of the country's most famous musicians is staying up all night with Joan Baez and Gordon Lightfoot, eating, drinking, and singing as the sun rose over her Carmel Valley home.

His father was Assyrian, his mother half Armenian, half Assyrian. His most distinguishing feature is a nose the size of a small car. It makes a perfect rest for the Leica M4s he carries everywhere. (He had five of them with him on the stage at Woodstock.)

Marshall is a loyal friend and a frightening enemy. All at the same time you want to put your arm around him, be seen with him, *and* be at another table or in another state when he threatens, loudly, to strangle the busboy for not keeping his water glass filled. He's a walking contradiction, his own worst enemy. The only certain thing about Marshall is his collection of photographs. They are a history of modern music, sensitive portraits and performance shots captured on twenty thousand rolls of carefully indexed Tri-X negatives. No one has a comparable body of work. But when the 1960s ended and the magic died, a big part of Jim Marshall died too. And it has proven tough to bring that magic back.

It's a late fall afternoon and Marshall is reclining on a redwood deck overlooking Carmel Valley. "Once," he says, "I was traveling with Creedence Clearwater Revival and they let me take their Lear jet from London to Geneva. I was going down to see a guy at *Camera* magazine. The plane landed and I walked out by myself. All these people standing around couldn't figure out if I was a rock and roll star or some Arab oil sheik. Took a limo to the magazine. I had about sixty bucks in my pocket."

Geneva is a long way from San Francisco's Fillmore District, where Marshall grew up, the son of a hard-drinking house painter who left home when Jim was ten, and a mother who supported the family working in a laundry. Marshall says he was always intrigued by mechanisms: guns, car engines, cameras. He and his friends made their first zip guns by adapting Kilgore cap pistols with steel tubing hollowed out to exactly .22 caliber. In high school he raced cars at the old Fremont Drag Strip and kept a scrapbook of pictures of cameras, pre-M series Leicas, Argus C3s. He sold motor scooters, served a couple of years in the air force, and worked as a claims adjuster for an insurance company. But he decided that what he really wanted to be was a photographer. In 1960 he put a down payment on a Leica M2 and paid it off in twelve monthly installments. He hung around North Beach, a copy of Camus in one pocket, Gibran in the other. He showed his meager portfolio around, got some work from a couple of California-based record companies, and met and photographed John Coltrane — strong, intimate photographs that bared a glimmer of the Marshall magic.

In 1962 the comedian Dick Gregory asked Marshall to drive his Thunderbird to Chicago for him. A bus took the photographer the rest of the way to New York, where he was going to "make my reputation, become famous and all that." He got a $100-a-month apartment on Charles Street in Greenwich Village. Bob Dylan lived around the corner, Judy Collins a couple of blocks away, the Lovin' Spoonful nearby. Marshall started hanging out, taking pictures in clubs, at recording sessions, and on the streets. Most of his work was for record companies — Atlantic, ABC, Impulse. Some was done for individual artists, and he got occasional assignments from a handful of magazines, including the *Saturday Evening Post*, *Look*, and *Escapade*. (The *Saturday Evening Post* also gave Marshall a nonmusic assignment, sending him to photograph the poor of Appalachia. His pictures never appeared in the magazine, but a year later eighteen of them turned up in a Smithsonian show called "Profiles in Poverty.") He shot in jazz clubs and at folk festivals. "Music was Jim's entire life," remembers Gahr.

After two years in New York Marshall figured he had the contacts he needed and moved back home. It was a shrewd decision. By 1965 all the world's musical attention had turned to rock & roll, and San Francisco was the music's mecca. "In those days," recalls Baron Wolman, *Rolling Stone*'s first chief photographer, "music was big news; we were breaking new ground, getting pictures people had never seen before. It was as big news as Vietnam, and everybody wanted pictures."

And everybody seemed to want Marshall's pictures. But he could be arrogant and pushy, in a business filled with arrogant and pushy people, and he rarely took no for an answer. "His style was to kick in the door and take what he could," says photographer Bob Siedemann, who was often right behind Marshall as the door fell down. "It didn't make him a lot of friends, but the music business is tough and Jim was tough. And people liked him anyway."

"There wasn't the pack photography that you see today," says Gahr. "We had unlimited access. One-on-one is how a photographer finds out if people have character, style. We got that kind of access in those days, and Marshall is great one-on-one."

Marshall photographed the famous and infamous young superstars of rock as people, not celebrities. Mick Jagger looking pensive; Janis Joplin smiling and weeping; Bob Dylan rolling a tire down Seventh Avenue; the Beatles readying for what would be their last concert together; Duane Allman tuning up in a Holiday Inn bathroom; Jimi Hendrix smiling devilishly into the camera seconds before he torched his guitar at Monterey. The artists trusted Marshall, and he

was backstage with them, in their hotel rooms, on their planes, in their homes. His own Union Street apartment became a salon of sorts, and musicians stopped by and wrote songs, drank whiskey, did drugs, had their pictures taken, and crashed.

"From 1963 to 1970 I was big time," Marshall says. "The phone was ringing all the time — managers, art directors wanting me to go here and there. There were times I just wouldn't answer the phone, I was so busy. One time it was George Harrison calling, about midnight. I didn't answer. Later I found out he had wanted me to shoot the Bangladesh concert."

By 1972 the scene had begun to change and success was taking its toll on the artists, and on Marshall. It was getting harder to get close to the musicians. And Marshall had developed quite a reputation — everything in excess. *Life* hired him to shoot that year's Rolling Stones tour for a cover story. Famed *Life* writer Tommy Thompson, assigned to the story, called the magazine's editors daily, demanding they banish this madman from the tour. With trepidation, the picture editor hung with Marshall, and his insightful pictures carried the story.

Over the course of the decade Marshall built a vast body of work and burned most of his bridges behind him. If he didn't get paid quickly enough, if he didn't like the way his pictures were used, he threatened art directors and editors with physical violence. If he didn't get the access to musicians he thought he deserved, he threatened promoters and managers. By 1972 his reputation preceded him everywhere. But everybody still loved the pictures in spite of the photographer.

Marshall figures his pictures are part of between five hundred and six hundred record/CD packages, on the cover, the back, or the sleeve. His favorite? The Allman Brothers' *At Fillmore East*. He likes it because of the myths that sprouted about the cover photo. "No, it wasn't taken in an alley in New York with guards hired to protect us from the Lower East Side crowd," says Marshall. "The front and back covers were taken in Macon, Georgia. The amp cases were all empty, and I stenciled 'The Allman Brothers Band At Fillmore East' on one of them with a can of white spray paint I bought at a hardware store. I had the only cocaine in Macon that day, and afterward we went out for fried chicken. Best fried chicken I ever had."

For about a decade, from 1974 to 1984, Marshall didn't take many pictures. The music scene had gone flat, and many of those Marshall loved — Jimi, Janis, Duane — were dead. His second wife, Becky, was making good money as a banker; he continued to sell prints to collectors and fans but withdrew behind the pulled blinds of his apartment. His friends were dope dealers and gun peddlers. "I handled the coke pretty well on that 'seventy-two tour [with the Rolling Stones], but after that I started doing more and more," says Marshall. "Not to just keep going, or get a little buzz. I wanted to do tons of it." He was busted for coke possession in 1975 and got probation.

In December 1981 he lost the last thread of stability he had. Becky left a note in his sock drawer explaining she couldn't take it anymore. Her divorce papers came in the mail from Minneapolis a year later. Fifteen months later, in March 1983, the violence swelled to a bursting point. A neighbor tripped the burglar alarm in Marshall's apartment, and Marshall rushed into the hall screaming obscenities and waving a .45 automatic in the woman's face. A week later a half-dozen cops were at his door, accompanied, luckily for Marshall, by a detective friend of his, who shouted a warning through the door. "If he hadn't been with them," says Marshall, "they would have probably just kicked the door down, and I'd have opened fire." That would have been the ignominious end to *the* rock & roll photographer. Instead it looked like five years in prison.

He did not go to prison in 1983; instead he qualified for work furlough. The local media had a heyday with his arrest, reporting that the police had seized over fifty pounds of armor-piercing bullets in their early morning raid. Marshall insists they got at most fifty of the bullets, plus $10,000 worth of weapons. For eight months he paid $4 a day to live in a barracks on Bryant Street and worked for $150 a week as an assistant to commercial photographer Dennis Gray. "I'd pick him up in the morning and drop him off at night," says Gray. "Having him around cost me three to four clients, just based on his reputation alone. But I was an admirer of his work and figured he deserved one more break. We struck a deal. He couldn't talk to my clients, he couldn't show them his work. And every once in a while I made him call me bwana." Marshall didn't mind that form of slavery, because even sweeping floors and random urine tests and metal bunk beds beat prison.

He was released from work furlough on February 4, 1984, one day after his forty-eighth birthday. Since then he's tried to present a new, calmer self, pursuing his grievances via the courts instead of with a gun. He's currently engaged in two lawsuits over unauthorized use of his pictures. See you in court, motherfucker, is Marshall's new coda.

The music business probably won't have Marshall back. He could never, or at least would never, do the kind of pictures in demand now. Think of his warm backstage pictures, then think of the assembly-line pictures that were taken behind the stage at Philadelphia's "Live Aid" concert in 1985, everybody posed in front of the same gray backdrop, emotionless. Record companies used to control the business; today managers call the shots. Photographers at concerts today are generally allowed to shoot only the first two to three songs, from a safe distance, and then they're hustled out the door. Control is the name of the game.

"I care so much about the music business that I don't care anymore," says Marshall. "I won't be part of a pack, I will not work that way." He bangs down his fist hard. "I've had fifty phone calls the last couple of years from people wanting to buy Springsteen prints. They assume I must have some. I don't got 'em. I won't shoot just two songs at a concert. They wouldn't be Jim Marshall pictures."

Marshall's rehabilitation process could have been easier, but he remains optimistic at sixty-one years old. Dennis Gray watched Marshall photograph Carlos Santana recently, though, and insists *the* rock & roll photographer still has the magic. His printer of twenty years, Kirk Anspach, says Marshall still "makes the best, sharpest negatives in town." Marshall is currently represented by Fahey/Klein Gallery in Los Angeles.

"I can adapt pretty well to a lot of different situations," says Marshall, "when I put my ego aside. When I decide to be the decent human being I'm capable of, I can get along real well. I'll be okay."

Marshall carries two lists in his wallet these days, scribbled on brown paper. One is of the artists he'd still like to photograph: Springsteen, Tom Petty, Dire Straits, Bette Midler, Smokey Robinson, Bob Seger, and David Bowie. The other is a list of his Top Ten all-time favorite seminal rock & roll songs. "Hungry Heart," "Rock Around the Clock," "Light My Fire," "Purple Haze," "Whiter Shade of Pale," "River Deep, Mountain High," "Satisfaction," "Like a Rolling Stone," "Bridge over Troubled Water," "For What It's Worth," and "I Want to Hold Your Hand." "Not a bad bunch of songs," he says, looking for confirmation. Always the enthusiast, overzealous to the end, Marshall's Top Ten boasts eleven songs.

Late one night Marshall and I show up at the entrance to the posh Venetian Room at the Fairmont Hotel. He is dressed in blue jeans and the threadbare corduroy coat that has become one of his trademarks. Three Leicas hang around his neck and off his shoulder. The tuxedoed maître d' gives him the once-over while Marshall explains he's here to photograph Oscar Peterson for the hotel's owner, a favor for an old friend.

The maître d' finally nods and shows Marshall to a table at the side of the room. "I'm sorry," Marshall says politely, "but this won't work." The maître d' gives in once more and guides the photographer to the best seat in the house, directly in front of Peterson's Bosendorfer piano. A complimentary Irish whiskey, a double, appears.

As the lights go down, the only sounds emanating from the photographer are his constant nervous finger picking and the heavy breathing of a large nose carved up from abuse. His cameras are silent. But as the music begins, so does Marshall. Between sets he describes it in terms of guns. "Waiting for the right shot onstage is like a sniper waiting for the target to be perfect. There's the same discipline. Steady, aim, focus, squeeze don't jerk." Another double whiskey is set in front of the photographer. He smiles, remembering some singular memory. "You know, when I had unlimited access, when the lighting was good and the music was right, there was no greater high. Man, I swear to God, it was unbelievable, there are no words to describe that feeling. The music washes away all the crap. There were nights . . . Coltrane took me to other planets. The Allman Brothers, Mahavishnu and Santana. Hendrix. Joan Baez a couple of nights. Pete Seeger. Johnny Cash at Folsom Prison. Good God, was I lucky."